Let's Explore

# Water

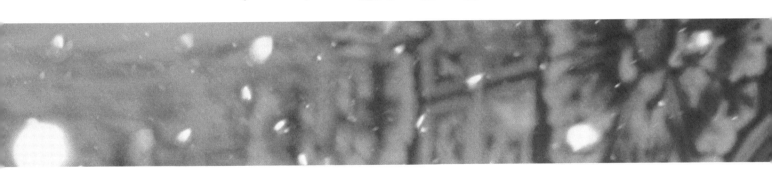

by Henry Pluckrose

**W**
FRANKLIN WATTS
LONDON•SYDNEY

# Author's note

This book is one of a series which has been designed to encourage young readers to think about the everyday concepts that form part of their world. The text and photographs complement each other, and both elements combine to provide starting points for discussion. Although each book is complete in itself, each title links closely with others in the set, so presenting an ideal platform for learning.

I have consciously avoided 'writing down' to my readers. Young children like to know the 'real' words for things, and are better able to express themselves when they can use correct terms with confidence.

Young children learn from the experiences they share with adults around them. The child offers his or her ideas which are then developed and extended through the adult. The books in this series are a means for the child and adult to share informal talk, photographs and text, and the ideas which accompany them.

One particular element merits comment. Information books are also reading books. Like a successful story book, an effective information book will be turned to again and again. As children develop, their appreciation of the significance of fact develops too. The young child who asks 'Where does water come from?' may subsequently and more provocatively ask, 'What happens if there is not enough water?' Thoughts take time to generate. Hopefully books like those in this series provide the momentum for this.

Henry Pluckrose

# Contents

Storm clouds 4

Rain 6

Mist 8

Drinking water 10

Keeping healthy 12

Running water 14

Frozen water 16

Evaporation 18

Dissolving in water 20

Floating 22

Animals in water 24

Water sports 26

Drought 28

Water pollution 30

Index 32

Why are the clouds
so heavy and dark?
They are full of
tiny drops of water.
The drops of water fall
from the clouds as rain.

Some of the rain soaks
into the ground.
Some of it flows
into gutters and drains.
It splashes into rivers and ponds.
It runs from rivers into the sea.

The rain stops. The sun shines.
Heat from the sun
makes the water evaporate
and turns it into mist.
It rises in the air
and forms new clouds.
Later it will fall again as rain.

Water is life-giving.
People, animals, plants
all need water to live.
Without water we would die.

When we breathe
we breathe out moisture.
When we are hot
we sweat and lose moisture.
We need to drink water
to keep healthy.

Water is usually a liquid.
The water in rivers and streams
flows downhill, into lakes,
seas and oceans.

When water gets very cold
it freezes into solid ice.
The north and south poles
are covered in ice
all the year round.

We can heat water until it boils
and turns into a vapour, or gas.
The steam coming
out of this kettle
is water that is
evaporating.

Many things dissolve in water.
What happens to sugar
when you stir it into water?

Many things float on water:
giant oil tankers,
pretty pleasure boats,
tiny canoes, leaves, twigs,
and even ducks...
The water holds them up.

Many animals and plants
live in or near the water.

# Why do water-birds have webbed feet?

Water sports are great fun.
You can go swimming,
surfing and water-skiing.
But always be very careful.
Deep water can be dangerous.

In some parts of the world, there is not enough water.

Crops do not grow.

Animals die.

People have nothing to eat.

We all need water to live.
We must make sure
that we care for
the water around us,
that we do not waste it
and do not pollute it.

# Index

animals  11, 24, 29

boats  22

clouds  5, 8

cold  16

dissolve  21

evaporate  8, 18

float  22

heat  8, 18

ice  16

lakes  14

liquid  14

moisture  13

oceans  14

plants  11

ponds  7

rain  5, 7, 8

rivers  7, 14

sea  7, 14

sports  26

steam  18

streams  14

water  5, 11, 13, 14, 16,
18, 22, 24, 25, 26,
29, 30

First published in 2000 by
Franklin Watts
96 Leonard Street
London
EC2A 4XD

Franklin Watts Australia
14 Mars Road
Lane Cove
NSW 2066

Copyright © Franklin Watts 2000

ISBN 0 7496 3822 2

Dewey Decimal
Classification Number 553.7

A CIP catalogue record for this book is
available from the British Library

**Series editor:** Louise John
**Series designer:** Jason Anscomb

Printed in Hong Kong

**Picture Credits:**
Still Pictures p.4 (Gunter Ziesler), p.10
(Martin Harvey), p.13 (John Isaac), p.28
(KITTPREMPOOL-UNEP), p.31 (F. Polking);
Images Colour Library pp.9, 15, 23, 25; Bruce
Coleman Collection p.17 (Francisco J Erize),
p.24 (Dr Scott Nielsen); Robert Harding p.6
(Raj Kamal); Tony Stone Images pp. 27, 32
and title page (George Kamper); Steve Shott
Photography pp. 20, 21; Ray Moller
Photography p.19.